"His STORY"

*The Prima Facie Case of **MURDER***
Against Dick Cheney, Donald Rumsfeld
*And the **SHADOW** Government*

9/11 THE PENTAGON MURDERS

Witten for ***ALL of the victims***

since September 11th, 2001

by Patrick Michael Alaggio

Avid Readers Publishing Group

Lakewood, California

Avid Readers Publishing Group

http://www.avidreaderspg.com

ISBN-13: 978-1-61286-333-7

Printed in the United States

"His Story" was written to expose the true murderers behind the attack on the Pentagon on September 11th, 2001. The information contained herein is based upon the reference sources provided within this document and the previous research done by this author over the last sixteen years. This has not only been a national tragedy but one that our NATION, without OUR *informed consent* but *IN OUR NAMES*, inflicted grievous harm to innocent victims around the world.

I ask that each reader cast away your predisposed verdict and examine the evidence as presented herein. You will read how both sides, the *"official"* government's story (*His STORY*) and the story supported by the FACTS as presented by the imaginary prosecution, which is a literary device I employed to make the vast amount of information easier to understand and absorb. When we are through with this presentation I will ask you to cast your verdict; **Innocent? Or, Guilty as charged!**

Patrick Michael Alaggio

http://www.palaggio.net

"Those who can be made to believe absurdities

can be made to commit atrocities!"

Voltaire

This work is lovingly dedicated to...

All who lost their lives; those injured and maimed, as well as their loved ones, the soldiers who have died either in combat or through suicides and to all who mourn alongside with them.

- *the victims*

- *their families*

- *the FIRST Responders*

- *the casualties of OUR wars*

- *and the innocence of ALL children from OUR Nation's SHAMEFUL Acts!*

"We the PEOPLE" are GUILTY of

whatever we let the government do

"IN OUR NAMES".

"In a time of universal deceit -

telling the truth is a revolutionary act."

George Orwell

INTRODUCTION:

The facts presented in this book are from credible, often expert witnesses that unanimously paint the **identical** picture. The government's *"evidence"* can be proven to be manufactured, falsified and conflicting. That's **when** the evidence is provided at all and NOT confiscated, destroyed and locked away under the guise of *"national security";* a term that this author has come to learn is synonymous with protecting the guilty within.

The conclusions and prosecutor's case are based upon the evidence provided herein as well as over fifteen years of research. Due to the complexity of four separate and distinct tragedies on September 11th, 2001 I have chosen to focus on only one aspect of that day's events in order to simplify the otherwise incomprehensible so we may PROVE GUILT beyond any reasonable doubt. We had: **1)** the World Trade Centers *(One **and** Two)*; **2)** the tragic crash of United Airlines Flight 93 / N591UA **3)** the **mysterious fall of BUILDING SEVEN** *(a 47 story tower that WASN'T HIT by a plane and still fell into its own footprint at **"nearly FREE FALL speed"**)*. For many of us it was Building 7 that provided the **SMOKING GUN**, especially when we saw it **still standing** in the background of a live British TV report speaking of that tragedy **BEFORE** IT OCCURED! **NOW THAT's REPORTING!** And of course **4) The Pentagon attack.**

These complexities overwhelm those of us who wish only to lead normal, peaceful lives. Those of us who wish to find and prosecute the guilty often find ourselves in conflict with our loved ones, our friends and those who blindly, in a false sense of patriotism, DEFEND THEIR COUNTRY against the likes of us, their fellow patriots and truth seekers. We are called *"conspiracy theorists"*, a derogatory term that was invented by the C.I.A. in 1967 to muffle those voices trying to get through the obvious inconsistencies of the Kennedy assassination; you know *"little things"*, like the *"magic bullet" theory*.

That is why I have chosen to focus **only** on the Pentagon attack. The epiphany came when I awoke with the answer to this puzzle firmly implanted in my head. How it got there would make a wonderful philosophical discussion but my intent is to scale this mystery down to a size that every intelligent person willing to keep an open mind can wrap their head around.

You will hear two theories; that provided by our government and that provided by the eyewitnesses, the researchers, the experts and most importantly, *the evidence!* So bring along your *"tin foil hats"* just in case you decide to vote guilty.

"When liars lead only cowards, accomplices and the feeble minded follow."

Patrick Alaggio

The PRIMA FACIE case against the parties named and/or indicated, are based upon the author's conclusions after a thorough review of the evidence. As of yet there has been no trial and we must presume innocence until guilt has been proven in a **LEGITIMATE** court of law. ***THAT IS THE PURPOSE OF THIS BOOK***; to bring to trial the accused, to identify their accomplices and to prosecute and, upon conviction, treat them accordingly; ***in exactly the same manner as the poorest among us would be treated.*** Without **EQUAL justice** there is only tyranny.

"The limits of tyrants are prescribed by the

endurance of those whom they oppress."

Frederick Douglas

The Mysterious Pentagon Attack of 9/11/2001:

PART 1: The government's *"BLACK HOLE THEORY"*

A. The FEDERAL government of the United States of America would have us believe that an unskilled pilot trained on a single engine **Cessna 172** could have driven his hijacked 757 commercial airliner into the Pentagon after implementing a **330 degree downward spiral at 465 knots** *(a ridiculously fast speed for a 757)*, **while descending** at the rate of **4,400 feet per minute** and, according to *THEIR* Flight 77's data recorder, *without having used the foot rudder pedals even once during the entire maneuver!*

NOTE: American Airlines 757 **"Flight 77"** was the SECOND time on that fateful day that a commercial aircraft exceeded its maximum operating speed by an outrageous amount. The first time was with the hijacked 767 that crashed into the first World Trade Center and was shown on radar to be travelling 150 knots over the maximum operating speed of that air-frame. See **"Pilot's for 9/11 Truth" documentary"**: **"9/11: INTERCEPTED"** at ~18:35 into this evidence. **Note:** A convenient outline can be found at **34:11** of that video presentation and also used to synch up various YouTube copies, which might have slight variations in the time stamp reference points I've provided.

Then, this amazing Cessna pilot was somehow able to defeat an *"aerodynamic physics barrier"* known as **GROUND EFFECT**, pulled up *just in time* to knock down five light poles *(driving the first pole through a taxi cab's windshield* **with astronomical force** *WITHOUT injuring the driver or leaving a single scratch on the hood of the car)*, attained level flight at 7 to 8 feet above the ground *(as per the tampered / photo shopped picture; see reference frame 23),* **without having scraped the ground** *(not even with that huge 8 foot tall 7,000 pound Rolls Royce RB211 engine that hung* **below** *the downward tilted left wing that was closest to the ground,* whereupon it proceeded to punch a **magical 16' to 20' black hole** into the outer "E" ring of the Pentagon that then **swallowed the entire 100 ton structure** *(and the light around it, which would explain the shocking lack of photographic evidence from the documented 86 cameras that* **SHOULD HAVE** *witnessed this event),* whereupon the entire 757 collapsed in upon itself, wings, titanium engines, horizontal stabilizers and tail fin **without leaving their marks on the walls of the Pentagon** *(where these physical structures would have* **definitely** *impacted the building)* **and WITHOUT leaving any significant wreckage on the outside lawn!**

There are far too many unanswered questions and provable fallacies that force us to put this poorly contrived story into the category of those told by our mother's when we were still innocent children. **Question:** Why, if the government's *"story"* was true was Purdue University's video simulation tampered with to remove that left engine from their presentation? **Answer:** Because it would have proven that the official "story" could not be substantiated by the physical evidence and was therefore not possible!

If this was a real plane crash then where were the *huge "nearly indestructible" titanium engines*, wings, horizontal stabilizers and tail fin? Where were the seats, bodies, luggage and large pieces of the plane's structure? Also, how was it possible that building support column **14AA** on the second floor *(that was in the center of this alleged impact hole)* **was left intact?** Why were the building support columns, where the wings would have impacted, *pushed upward and OUT* as opposed to having been driven inward from that 200,000 pound projectile? Why was there so little foundation damage where this huge planes 7,000 pound titanium engine would have impacted? Why did the FBI immediately confiscate ALL of photographic *evidence* in the area? Why, when they finally did release a tiny fraction of this evidence did they provide only two short snippets *(from two closely positioned cameras)* that upon expert evaluation PROVED that even this minute amount evidence had been tampered with! **Note:** Present frame 23 and photo shop expert.

According to the *"official story"* this gigantic plane, upon impact with the Pentagon, simply collapsed neatly in upon itself and proceeded inward through that fuselage sized hole. We are TOLD to believe the huge air frame miraculously folded up and squeezed itself into that 16' to 20' hole without leaving a significant trace on the lawn; whereupon, it continued through the Pentagon's inner "D" and "C" rings leaving a nearly perfect 8 to 10 foot circle where the nose cone allegedly poked through. There were no skid marks on the lawn and only small debris items that were easily picked up by hand.

When you study the evidence provided by **Pilots for 9/11 Truth** and that obtained by a Freedom of Information Subpoena that forced the release of the plane's flight data recorder *(i.e. "black box")*, you will find many more amazing facts and additional distortions that make the government's THEORY not only improbable but physically and mathematically impossible! *(Just like the Warren Commission's* **"magic bullet"** *theory during that particular cover up on the JFK assassination fifty-four years ago!)* **NOTE:** This gives us an opportunity to remember and to teach George Santayana's warning; *"Those who fail to study history will be condemned to repeat it."* Well, "we the people" have been studying!

For example;

1) **EXPERT commercial pilots** looked at the radar evidence and said it was an impossible maneuver for an amateur pilot and only seasoned professional pilots could have executed it.

2) Why pull that extremely difficult **330 degree descending spiraling maneuver** in the first place when flying directly into the building would have been much easier?

3) The point of alleged impact at the Pentagon was the EXACT spot where the civilian accountants, bookkeepers and auditors were busy at work trying to find the "**2.3 TRILLION DOLLARS that went missing from the Pentagon budget**" as announced by **Secretary of Defense Donald Rumsfeld on September 10th; THE DAY BEFORE the 9/11 attacks!**

4) According to the experts the rate of descent along with the last moment *"pull-up maneuver"* to level flight **could not have been accomplished without structural failure to the air-frame!**

5) Final point for the moment; in the radar images, long before Washington DC had become a known target, there were two mysterious planes doing a **"do-si-doe"** *(a square dance term when partners*

lock elbows and swing in a circle) with two of the "hijacked" airliners and then the new planes took the flight path of the hijacked commercial jets and the original American Airline jets LANDED SAFELY out of the public view. *(See following note...)* This is shown on the radar images and it is important to recognize that this *"maneuver"* was WHEN the airliners were replaced with remote controlled military DRONE planes *(that did not look the same as reported by many witnesses)* and had a maximum operating flight speed that far exceeded that of the commercial airliner jets they replaced. This would explain how the unbelievable speeds that were documented on radar could have been attained.

NOTE: This murderous episode closely approx-imated the one recommended to President John F. Kennedy in 1962 by the Department of Defense (DoD) and the Joint Chiefs of Staff with the now declassified **"Operation Northwood's"** document. This information was released from secret documents obtained from FREEDOM OF INFORMATION subpoenas. In that 1962 *black operations plot* drones were to be used against *our own people* to blame on Castro in order to garner support of THEIR efforts against his regime. President Kennedy refused to allow this treachery to take place.

NOTE: See **"Pilot's for 9/11 Truth" documentary"**: **"9/11: INTERCEPTED"** at ~16:50 into this evidence and a little further showing the documented *"do-si-do maneuver"* on radar between TWO sets of aircraft, one set of the hijacked American Airline planes *(and the most likely scenario)* of remotely controlled military aircraft that replaced these aircraft and then continued on to their ***designated targets!***

This is a brief sample of the government's *"official story"* plus a few discrediting facts from our research, which we will get much further into in PART 2. I'm sure we will all look forward to THEIR upcoming justifications to these accusations but I forewarn THEM that *"we the people"* are no longer naïve nor will we believe in mystical fairy tales as with ***the magic bullet theory***.

13

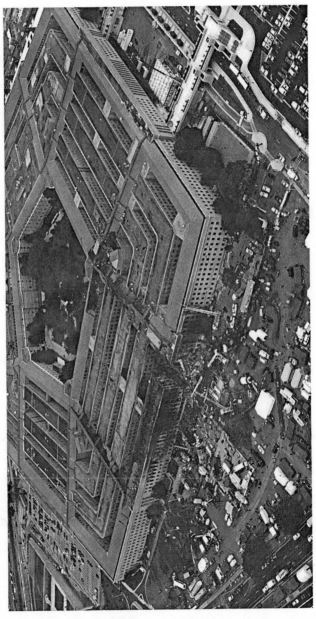

19

M-CSP-00001567

20

The Mysterious Pentagon Attack of 9/11/2001:

PART 2: *The Prosecution's Case for* <u>*MURDER*</u> *AGAINST Dick Cheney, Donald Rumsfeld and the SHADOW Government.*

Ladies and gentlemen; I am not a lawyer nor am I an explosives expert. I am merely one of millions of concerned citizens that have *refused* to accept the official story put out by our government concerning the attacks that occurred on September 11, 2001. In this report I have focused on only one aspect of those attacks; **American Airlines Flight 77 / N644AA**, which was a **757** (model 223) commercial airliner that departed Washington/Dulles Airport at 8:30 am, disappeared off of radar over West Virginia when it was *allegedly* hijacked and then flown into the Pentagon at 9:37 am... *ONE HOUR AND SEVEN MINUTES AFTER TAKE OFF.*

I have chosen NOT to simply report my findings to you but to provide this courtroom scenario and ask each of you to become a member of the jury. The primary reason is because I believe it will be more interesting and easier to understand and absorb this information. I have studied all aspects of the 911 tragedy since discovering the collapse of World Trade Center 7 *(a 47 story building)*, the THIRD skyscraper to fall in NYC and **WAS NOT** hit by a plane. We will focus primarily on the Pentagon attack in order to prove murder without making this aspect of the case overwhelmingly complicated. By taking a laser sharp focus on just the Pentagon *"we the people"* can make a strong case for MURDER against Vice-President Dick Cheney, Secretary of Defense Donald Rumsfeld and others within the military-industrial-complex, the F.B.I., the C.I.A. and the National Security Agency.

Of course there will be many more, such as those who hid the truth from us in the media and are therefore complicit. However, for this exercise I only wish to FIRMLY ESTABLISH the need to make arrests and begin high-level prosecutions by presenting what I know will soon be seen as irrefutable PROOF of an *INSIDE JOB* conducted by our own government against the citizens of the United States of America. As a fellow citizen, father and PATRIOT *I cannot and will not let this treason stand!*

When you look at the government's case in defense of our charges you are going to sense confusion where the pieces just don't seem to fit. We will show you how they have lied and then how they have amplified their own fallacies with even more lies that contradict their previous "story".

In order to simplify THEIR purposeful deceit I want you to imagine being given **FOUR** different puzzles to put together. Now, instead of being given each of these puzzles with a picture on the box of what it is supposed to look like when completed; imagine you are given all of the pieces turned upside down so all that can be seen is the cardboard backing and not the colors and hues, which act as clues, guides and hints as to which pieces might fit together. Now let's consider which puzzle is easier to put together; 1) the first being the way a child would put it together, picture sides up and studying the completed picture on the box for clues as to how to proceed; or, 2) that same puzzle without a picture to go by; or, 3) that same puzzle without a picture to go by and with all of the pieces turned upside down. Now which of these puzzles do you think would be finished first, second and third by three equally talented people?

Now, imagine you have been gifted with FOUR puzzles and that those puzzles were combined into ONE HUGE PILE and that ALL of the pieces had been turned upside down exposing only cardboard. Then throw in another couple hundred fake puzzle pieces to make the solution even more difficult by adding yet another layer of complexity and confusion.

That, ladies and gentlemen is why the attacks of September 11th, 2001 have been so confusing and difficult to understand for so long. It also helps explain why so many of our friends and loved ones have simply given up and moved on with their lives and no longer wish to discuss this any further, which is exactly what the government wants us to do; for *"we the people"* to give up and let them get away with their atrocities.

However, for those who lost loved ones, friends and their sense of innocence, safety and freedom; moving on and simply letting go of this tragedy has never been an option. Those of us who have spent countless hours mourning, praying and researching will never give up until ALL of the puzzles are solved. Instead we bemoan each and every obvious lie and then claw at it relentlessly until that piece can be turned over and shared with the rest of our 9/11 *"family"*. We take every bone of contention and dig at it like some ravenous dog until a scrap of evidence proves true or at least proves the lie, which then allows us to place it into the ever growing garbage heap; and then again, we turn that piece over and share it with one another... piece by piece, year after year... sixteen years and counting.

We, the 9/11 family of TRUTH SEEKERS, who we have been discourteously called **"TRUTHER's"** by the main stream media, wear THEIR derogatory badge with HONOR and WE intend to get to the bottom of all of these puzzles and to extract justice, but not all at once. Today we are only going to look at the last puzzle, the Pentagon attack, so we may prove beyond any reasonable doubt, that those killed inside of the Pentagon were in fact **purposefully targeted** and then murdered by those identified in this report and those in the SHADOW government lurking within the military-industrial-intelligence complex and THEIR friend in the **main stream media** who continually help them to cover up these atrocities.

This 9/11 atrocity was planned from beginning to end. Any time you hear information being added that is outside of the scope of the Pentagon attack I want you to listen closely but then simultaneously put that piece into the appropriate puzzle box so it can be addressed at the proper time when those prosecutions are brought forth. For now, the attack on the Pentagon is the reason we are all here. Thank you for your attention.

At this point the Attorney for the defense would get up and tell you what they have been telling us for the last sixteen years. They would then call this a *"conspiracy theory"* but **NOT the FACT** that this derogatory term was *invented by the C.I.A. in 1967* to muffle those who spoke out about the Kennedy assassination. This terminology has been used ever since along with such descriptors as *"tin foil hat wearing" conspirators*, which is simply trying to add insult to injury. I will grant them the fact that my account of this factual evidence is indeed *my conspiracy theory!* I will then point out to you the extreme amount of flaws in what I have dubbed *the government's BLACK HOLE Theory*. When the prosecution rests there will be overwhelming evidence to prove THEIR culpability in this single slice of this murderous multi-tiered plot. The other slices of the mystery **WILL FOLLOW** as a result of the successful prosecution of this specific case. When we hear the voices of expert witnesses, we need to set aside our innocence, our normalcy biases and our naiveté in order to understand the truth as it really exists and not how we were taught as children to believe. Only then will we begin the long overdue process of prosecuting the massive crimes that have been waged against us since the murder of President John F Kennedy on November 22nd, 1963. It is long past time for us to recapture our stolen Constitutional Republic and our Bill of Rights from those who wish to destroy them.

At this point I need to point you to three very important YouTube presentations where the facts I am about to present can be verified with your own eyes and ears. If you do not have a computer or network connection handy don't worry. I will explain the facts clearly enough and provide the URL's (links) to the information along with the time stamps so you can double check this information at a more convenient time.

Here are the three specific presentations I would like you to open up in separate windows on your computer so you can quickly view the specific information as it is presented:

1. **9/11 The Impossible Case of Flight 77 (ref: "V1")**

   - https://www.youtube.com/watch?v=x779N003mHA

2. **911 INTERCEPTED (ref: "V2")** by Pilot's for 9/11 Truth

   - https://www.youtube.com/watch?v=reER-XWOHlE&t=3s

3. **911 Pentagon Flight Recorder Fraud Revealed (ref: "V3")**

by Dennis Cimino.

   - https://www.youtube.com/watch?v=mmGi5YeQ_Bw

Before we dig in let's take one minute to remember what Donald Rumsfeld, then Secretary of Defense, told us on the day *before the 911 attacks:*

"According to some estimates we cannot track 2.3 Trillion dollars in transactions." This CBS news broadcast *(link shown below)* went on to say: **"2.3 TRILLION, with a "T"!"** The VERY NEXT DAY those involved in the auditing of those lost funds were murdered along with the evidence they had compiled. Not too surprisingly that headline managed to get sidelined by the attacks of 9/11 and those trillions of stolen tax dollars, that went missing from the Pentagon budget, have not been given the attention it deserves- including the ongoing thefts; except, of course by those of us willing to don our tin foil hats and remain actively engaged.

See:

https://www.youtube.com/
watch?v=IVpSBUgbxBU

At this point, I would be asking for our first expert witness. May we have **Major General Albert Stubblebine** take the stand? In his last command this **expert witness** was in charge of **all of the Army's strategic intelligence forces around the world**, which included signals intelligence, photo intelligence, counter intelligence & human intelligence. When asked in the **"V1"** interview (at ~ 48:55 of that documentary) *"What hit the Pentagon?"* He states, and I QUOTE: *"I don't know exactly what hit it, but I do know, from the photographs that I have analyzed and looked at very, very carefully, it was not an airplane."* General Stubblebine goes on to say that *"our free press is no longer FREE; it is __VERY__ Expensive,* (repeating) *it is VERY expensive! The Press is saying what it has been TOLD TO SAY."*

So, if it was not an airplane then what was it? Let's continue...

When looking at a chain of events it is only logical and natural to look at them from beginning to end, A to Z. In this case that would mean the plane's departure, hijacking and (alleged) collision into the Pentagon's outer **"E"** ring. Unfortunately, when you look at it that way there are so many "anomalies" that simply don't make sense or add up, that the story remains a confused mess.

28

1. Where the HECK is the plane?

2. Why is the hole in Pentagon so small?
   (*16' to 20'* per pro-videographer Bob Pugh)

3. Where the HECK are the three sets of wing marks that should have been present on the building; from the huge 185 foot wide primary wings, the horizontal stabilizers and tail, which stood 24 feet above the fuselage of the plane?

4. How long after the original hole was punched in did the roof collapse and create that huge amount of damage?

5. Why is column **14AA** still intact if a 100 ton airplane hit it?

6. Why are there steel beams that are blown ***"up and outward"*** (towards the "E" ring lawn) instead of being pushed in by this huge projectile traveling at great speed?

For the longest time *"we the people"* had to struggle with these inconsistencies and many, including me, thought that a missile might have hit the building, which would answer some of these questions but NOT ALL of them. But then there were the other anomalies that arose if that had been the case.

7. Why, would the 5 light poles have fallen if this were a missile with a very narrow wing span?

Simple answer: ***They wouldn't have been hit!***

So it's back to square one and on top of all of the other anomalies in New York City, in Shanksville, Pennsylvania and 24 by 7 news coverage on every TV channel spewing out the government's STORY we were overwhelmed with information. Since this isn't a court of law I will call it for what it was; ***we were baffled with bovine excrement!*** Let's continue:

The government used the five light poles outside the Pentagon to prove to us that the plane had indeed approached from that direction, which was SOUTH of Columbia Turnpike. However, thirteen credible eyewitnesses swore within weeks of the event (to the **Library of Congress** or to the **Center for Military History** and then again in 2006 when interviewed by the ***Citizen Investigation Team*** who provided us with the **"V1"** video, ***that the airplane had in fact approached from the NORTH side of Columbia Turnpike***, which would have made the government's story not only **false** but IMPOSSIBLE! (Again see **"V1".**)

FOR THE RECORD here is a partial list of these witnesses regarding this point:

<u>**The eye witnesses interviewed and referenced were:**</u>

- **Vantage Point #1** (South Side of the Navy Annex):

    - Edward Paik – auto mechanic

    - **Terry Morin** – Program Manager Sparta Inc., an aviator who qualifies as an **EXPERT WITNESS**

    - **Chadwick Brooks** – Pentagon Police Officer – an **EXPERT WITNESS**

    - **William Lagasse** – Pentagon Police Officer – an **EXPERT WITNESS**

- **Vantage Points #2, 3, 4 and 5:**

    (See V1's overhead slide at ~32:54 for locations:)

    - Robert Turcios

    - Darius Prather

    - Donald Carter

    - Darrell Stafford

    - William Middleton

    - **Sean Boger – Pilot / Expert Witness**

Meanwhile, the *official* government story, as provided by the **9/11 Commission Report** in July of 2004, showed an *animation* of Flight 77 approaching the Pentagon from the **SOUTH** SIDE of Columbia Turnpike, *which was necessary in order* *to match the damage shown by the five fallen light posts and the entry point* into the Pentagon. The problem with this perspective is that the real data, as provided by another *simulation (years later)* from the **National Transportation Safety Board** (NTSB) showed those light poles would have been *far below* and to the south (right) of the flight path as allegedly indicated by the Flight Data Recorder of American Airlines Flight 77. This is where Mr. Dennis Cimino's *expert* testimony comes in and can be seen in detail in **"V3"**.

So, here we have two SIMULATIONS from the government showing their two completely different STORIES on FLIGHT 77's approach, one to match the downing of the five light poles approach (from the South of Columbia Turnpike) and one to match the EXPERT WITNESS TESTIMONY approach from the **North** of Columbia Turnpike as verified in 2006 by the **Citizen's Investigation Committee** interviews with the witnesses as presented in **"V1"** <u>*and as they originally testified*</u> to either the **Library of Congress** or **The Center for Military History** only weeks or a few months after the 9/11/2001 tragedy.

NOTE: We should pause for a moment to recognize that *ALL of the eyewitness testimony remained consistent!* The plane that everybody saw *approached the Pentagon from the NORTH SIDE of Columbia Turnpike,* which made it impossible for it to hit ANY of light poles!

Expert Witness **Dennis Cimino ("V3")** examined Flight 77's "black box" *(flight data recorder)* that was provided to him and was *"supposedly"* authentic. Here are some of his findings. **1)** that data recorder was NOT assigned with the planes **Identification number** or **flight number** and in those areas only zeroes appeared, which in layman's terms means this was a ***BENCH UNIT for testing*** and NOT READY FOR USE. By overriding the REQUIRED ID numbers in software the unit could still function, be tested, programmed and used as it was, ***to deceive us!*** **2)** According to this black box the alleged hijacking took place ***WITHOUT the door to the cockpit ever being opened***; another neat trick. **3)** Also according to this suspicious *"black box"*; this Flight Data Recorder showed that all of the maneuvers *(from the time it was reacquired on radar over West Virginia),* **including the rapid descent at 4,400 feet per minute and the 330 degree turn** that put the jet onto its final approach towards the Pentagon ***ALL OCCURRED WITHOUT THE FOOT PEDALS BEING TOUCHED*** *(not even once)*; another nifty trick!

So here we have another group of anomalies in the government's STORY. They told us that Flight 77 was heading west and was over West Virginia when the hijackers took control of the airliner; they did it without opening the cockpit door, they then disappeared from radar and a short while later and reappeared heading EAST and barreling its way back towards the Washington, DC area.

NOTE: When Flight 77 was *"reacquired"* it was against ALL KNOWN FAA protocols when a plane has fallen off the radar as Flight 77 had. Furthermore, as it maneuvered towards the Pentagon a radar air traffic controller, **Danielle O'Brien**, who had been watching this flight on her radar screen, told the press *"that it maneuvered like a military plane and NOT a commercial airliner because of the WAY it maneuvered and its excessive speed."*

It's important to understand that Washington DC has a *"prohibitive air space"* primarily around the White House and the Pentagon that is heavily protected in what is known as a **"CLASS BRAVO AIR SPACE".** This defensive designation is intended to identify and respond to any suspected hijacked or unidentified planes **that are not on a normal "preapproved" approach** *(as previously identified on their flight plans)* to the three airports in that immediate area. These NON-AUTHORIZED aircraft **WILL ALWAYS BE INTERCEPTED BY TWO JET FIGHTERS**, one that pulls next to the unidentified pilot and tries to communicate via radio *(or hand signals if necessary)*, while positioned just off the wing, as the second pilot circles the plane in case drastic actions need to be taken. This is their **NORMAL PROCEDURE** and is especially true for a hijacked 757 that weighs in at approximately 100 tons! It should have been intercepted, which is a routinely executed duty performed by these pilots many times each year.

Enter the government's testimony that they had their (phony) drills scheduled for the exact day as this attack; part of which had our pilots out over the Atlantic Ocean or chasing false blips on radar screens, which were used in THEIR plot to hide the treachery of that day. Once again we must ask; **REALLY?   ANOTHER COINCIDENCE?** *(I guess Osama Bin Laden was a mystic with amazing extra-sensory powers...)*

NOTE: Just like the Secret Service stood down **at multiple levels** during the JFK assassination our entire air force was unable to intercept airliners??? Proving Santayana's wisdom yet one more time; **"Those who cannot remember the past are con-demned to repeat it."**

Now this is where **Norman Mineta's** testimony factors in. He was the **Secretary of Transportation** at that time and while in the PEOC witnessed the following. A Navy Adjutant was in and out updating Vice-President Cheney on the approaching aircraft while they were in the **Presidential Emergency Operations Center**, which is a bunker that lies under the East Wing of the White House and serves as a secure shelter and communications center for the President in case of an emergency.
Secretary Mineta recalled the Officer reporting to VP Cheney: **"The plane is now 50 miles out... The plane is now 30 miles out..."** and when it got down to where the plane was 10 miles out the Navy Adjutant asked the Vice President: **"Do the order**

still stand?" According to Transportation Secretary Mineta: "Cheney whipped his head around and said: *OF COURSE THE ORDER STILL STAND! Have you heard anything to the contrary?"*

So there is our VP, effectively acting as President while George W. Bush reads to the children and **is never whisked away by the secret service while OUR country was under massive attack!** Now what did *our illustrious leader* Dick Cheney do, the acting commander and chief? NOTHING, Nadda, ZILCH, to intercept a known and long-tracked incoming threat to the one of the most secure airspaces in the WORLD!

For me this also begs the question; was President Bush a co-conspirator or a hostage? *Go along or we will kill you TOO!* Whatever George W. Bush was at that moment it WASN'T the president of the United States!

So as you can see this entire government *"story"* doesn't make any sense because it's a TOTAL fabrication and one big bag of horse droppings. If it seems unnecessarily confusing then recognize the fact that this is part of THEIR **PSYOPS AGENDA**; *lie, destroy evidence, obfuscate, propagandize...* then *repeat!* We're not even close to being done with these sociopaths yet!

While we are on this particular point it is worth mentioning that there is yet another layer of defense within this area known as the *"Basic Point Defensive Missile System"*, which are pop-up launchers with self-contained radar systems that appear on roof tops upon a verified threat and lock onto targets in a matter of seconds. These defenses can easily take down an airliner and are positioned where they are because of other buildings in this area are also considered **STRATEGIC TARGETS**. In other words, **IF THIS WERE AN <u>UNKNOWN</u> THREAT THESE POTENTIAL TARGETS WOULD HAVE BEEN PROTECTED AND THE THREAT SHOT DOWN!**

NOTE: The fighter pilots carry the *preauthorized authority to make the shoot down decision themselves*, without hesitation. If the pilot of the suspect plane doesn't follow the instructions given by the fighters then they become *legitimate TARGETS.*

Instead, what happens in this instance, AFTER we already knew of the attacks in New York City? The plane is allowed *(by Dick Cheney and his accomplices)* to fly <u>right past the White House</u>, *where agents on the roof could have shot down the plane with standard shoulder held STINGER MISSILES two or three times over!* Two more STAND DOWNS; sure why not!

Alright, we're NOT in a court of law so I am going to cut to the chase and speak the way I NEED TO and I've done my absolute best not to use profanities so our students can read this!

Our human nature has us looking at this whole fiasco from the wrong perspective *and that is on purpose from the sociopathic criminals that created this multifaceted plot against us.* You don't believe our wonderful leaders would do something like that? Then take a moment to actually read the **Operation Northwood's** plot. When you do you will see the DoD's declassified plan to use military drones to attack Americans in order to get the backing of OUR people for their desired aggressions against Cuba and Fidel Castro. Now if you recall I told you that this was all the way back in 1962! We had that capability then and I can assure you we have a far greater capabilities today FIFTY-FIVE YEARS later!

Since that time I have indirectly witnessed the murders of our President John F, Kennedy, Martin Luther King Jr., Malcom X and probable-President Bobby Kennedy. I've also witnessed the results of those murders; the Vietnam War; which JFK was committed to withdrawing from by the end of 1965 BEFORE it got ramped up by Lyndon Baines Johnson and the military-industrial-complex... but that's a prosecution for another day. The point *IS* however, if we don't stop them somewhere then we are going to be writing blank checks to these bastards until the end of time. Checks they will use to enslave our children.

So let me tell you what we are going to do. *We are going to STOP THESE PSYCHOPATHS AND*

SOCIOPATH'S RIGHT NOW! And we are going to do it by getting into their pathological heads, thinking the way sociopaths think and walking in their $1,000 sociopath shoes.

First we need to ask the universal question? **Cui bono?** *Who benefits?* Surely not we the people, the families or our loved ones... Surely not the ancient tribes in the Middle East who have had to endure the wrath of our military might for GOD knows how long? *(Sixteen years and counting!)* So REALLY, we are supposed to believe that this event pulled off by a rich terrorist living in a cave in AFHANISTAN? *Really?*

Alright, I needed that to get rile up enough to think like these monsters. You know people like Dick Cheney, Donald Rumsfeld and *ALL OF THEIR ACCOMPLICES!*

Let me give you some real motives that actually make sense:

1. THEY wanted a boost to the military-industrial-complex, but our people hate war... so what do THEY do?

2. THEY needed a way to dust off the existing plans to THEIR huge *"PATRIOT ACT"* so THEY could destroy OUR freedoms and remove us as a barrier to the globalist's plan for THEIR *"NEW WORLD ORDER"* as spoken of by President George H.W. Bush and the

rest of the traitors to our Constitution. Of course that was BEFORE many of us knew what that FASCIST declaration meant! Well ladies and gentlemen; *WE'RE NOT THAT INNOCENT OR NAÏVE NOW!*

3. THEY needed a way to justify THEIR planned illegal wars of aggression so THEY could steal the wealth of the Eurasian Continent using our vast military advantage. After all, THEY ask THEMSELVES; *"what's the point of having all of this power if we aren't going to use it?"* That's the way THEY think to HELL with collateral damages. But these planners were advised that the American people wouldn't go along with a war agenda, and they were correct, *UNLESS*, *(ah yes)* *unless* *(it's twirl the handle-bar mustache time)* THEY WERE GIVEN *"a catalyzing event, something on the scale of a new Pearl Harbor"* in order to motivate the people to support the upcoming wars *(that were already planned)* with a patriotic fervor. That little tidbit of truth was in the 9/11/2000 plan put out by the **Project for a New American Century** (PNAC) a think tank for the globalists. **Note:** Now you know how they got the name **"The Patriot Act"** don't you? Go back and read Orwell's **1984** and you will recognize they ARE using Orwellian **doublespeak.** In OUR **truthful language** it would have been called **The Enslavement**

Act! Then read Zbigniew Brzezinsky's **"The Grand Chessboard"**, which was written in 1997 and you will see that THEIR plans were laid out for our invasions many years in advance of 9/11. That gave them plenty of time to figure out **WHAT ELSE THEY COULD DO DURING THIS MASSIVE INSIDE JOB FALSE FLAG....** Hmmm, let's see.

4. THEY could steal the 100 billion dollars of gold out of the vaults under the World Trade Center Bank...

5. THEY could steal hundreds of billions of dollars in Bearer Bonds and diamonds that were held there too...

6. THEY could destroy Building 7, where over 3,600 high-level Securities and Exchange Commission investigations were under way. Without any records what could "we the people" do to prosecute the criminal elite? *There they go again; destroying evidence!*

7. They could DESTROY two asbestos ridden mega-structures, AKA "The TWIN TOWERS" that could not be economically brought up to code.

8. They could use the position and stature of Larry Silverstein to buy those WTC leases, insure those buildings for $125 million,

with specific language concerning terrorist attacks and double indemnity, only weeks ahead of the incident and allow him to receive over **$7 BILLION DOLLARS** in an insurance scam that surpasses even the one done by J.P. Morgan and the White Star Line when the Titanic *allegedly* sunk. (Another truth to be told at another time.) I know I said I wouldn't get into the other aspects of the 9/11 events but this is important because ALL OF THESE MOTIVES belong to the SAME conspiracy and are ALL part of the ACUMULATING MOTIVES even though we are only pushing on the Pentagon attack domino at this phase.

9. Now, the most important motive relative to the Pentagon Attack of September 11th, 2001. *(FOLLOW THE MONEY.)* That (alleged) plane impacted where? I already told you; the ONE-HUNDRED and TWENTY-FIVE civilian contractors (accountants, bookkeepers and auditors) who were tasked with finding the missing 2.3 TRILLION DOLLARS as told to us by Secretary of Defense DONALD RUMSFELD *the day before* the attacks. So, while THEY are already planning on murdering thousands of people in New York City... WHY NOT kill another few hundred and get rid of the evidence of **THEIR GIGANTIC HEIST**, one that is ongoing and currently amounts to

TENS of TRILLIONS of dollars stolen...

So there are just a few motives for you, off the top of my head, but now it's time to nail the coffin shut on these traitors.

Are you ready?

One nice thing about George Orwell is that he told us what was coming long before THEY actually implemented it. After seeing all the evidence, all the conflicts, lies, misdirection DOUBLE-SPEAK I realized that the solution to the Pentagon Attack lay not at the beginning, with the hijackers, but at the END, **<u>with the murderers</u>**! **"War is peace"**; remember doublespeak? How about: **"first is last"**, or better still, **"LAST IS FIRST"**. Then came the recently released picture of the unexplainable nearly-perfect circle-hole on the **INNER WALL** of the **"C"** ring of the Pentagon... **a place where only THEY had access to.**

"WHAT IF" that event didn't END there, as the aftermath of a plane crash**, but in REALITY, IT BEGAN THERE!** That makes more sense than THEIR STORY; that the soft nose cone of an aircraft, which is virtually hollow, survived the collision and penetrated through all of the steel beams, desks, walls of the E, D and C rings to punch out a nearly perfectly circular 10' to 12' hole on the inner most "C" ring wall? **Wow, that some mighty fine aluminum!**

THEY, the SHADOW government, led by Dick Cheney and Donald Rumsfeld and ALL of THEIR accomplices had a target, a motive and an opportunity! There was PHYSICAL evidence and testimonial evidence that couldn't be destroyed or stand the light of day once "we the people" took that *one additional step upward and onto the last set of researchers shoulders* to see just a little farther than the tens of thousands of researchers who came before, when I saw something just a little differently. *The exit wound was in fact an entrance wound that was designed, aimed and fired* into that innocent mass of humanity.

So, let's look <u>BACKWARDS</u> into this specific event and see if the facts fit any better; do they explain the anomalies, do they add up? If this were OUR plan to pull off what might we do?

Identify mission objectives;

- First, THEY knew *WHO* the targets were; the innocents trying to find **OUR** money.

- THEY knew *WHERE* the targets were and *WHEN* they would all be there.

So, how do you kill 125 people and get away with it?

You plant a *SHAPED EXPLOSIVE CHARGE* that was designed to kill every man, woman and child in the accounting department, which left that nearly perfect hole in the INNER "C" Ring wall of the MOST SECURE BUILING IN THE WORLD! *(I can almost hear the planner using his dark humor to sell his idea to his fellow TRAITORS using the JFK scenario; where they conducted a tracheotomy our deceased President who already had 30% of his brain blown out of the **back of his head**. Why? To hide the tiny entrance wound to the front of his throat... the ENTRANCE WOUND IN HIS THROAT. The old timers must have gotten a chuckle out of that! (I didn't!)* Now, they didn't know that in this moment of acceptance of this strategy that THEIR crime would inevitably become known. What they DID NOT realize is that this plan put them into a box from which there was no escaping the truth. *A box I prefer to think of as THEIR coffin.*

Once the starting point is understood we can follow the chain of events backwards and explain ALL of the anomalies that, until this point, have remained puzzling enough to provide THEM with *"plausible deniability"*. It's time to stand THEM up naked in front of the world and deny them even that shroud, which we will reserve for THEIR mass burial, preferable in one gigantic unmarked grave with a single tombstone reading;
"TRAITORS ALL!"

- The first part of the puzzle is in place. We now understand HOW the circular hole could have been created. OUR Theory; It was a shaped explosive charge of immense capability that was specifically designed to kill the accounting experts who were witnessing where the multi-trillion dollar theft and the whereabouts of that money trail. GOAL: Obliterate all of the evidence.

- This theory ALSO explains why there was no 757 at the alleged crash site.

- This theory ALSO explains why column **14AA**, that was in the middle of where the alleged 200,000 pound plane _would have collided_ with the Pentagon was left **intact**.

- This theory ALSO explains why the steel columns were blown UP and OUWARD towards the outside of the Pentagon. Towards the lawn and not shoved **into** the hole.

- This theory ALSO explains why the employees were never told of the NYC attacks OR warned of an incoming threat.

- This theory ALSO explains why the plane was never intercepted or shot down.

- This theory ALSO incorporates the **Operation Northwood's** aspect of the attack upon one's own people BUT **DOES NOT ADDRESS the actual plane itself,** which I will do shortly.

So there we have seven anomalies explained by simply starting at **Z** and working towards **A** and we are just getting started...

Now let's address the **FIVE downed light poles** and: **"The mysterious incident involving Mr. Lloyde England and his miraculous survival after colliding with light pole #5:**

This is where the murder plot found the conspirators trapped inside their own box. Once the target was known, the size and contents of the area that needed to be destroyed had been ascertained then any number of explosive experts could have designed the charge to be detonated. More than likely there were multiple experts all answering this same **TEST QUESTION** without having the faintest idea of what is was needed for. Perhaps all they wanted was an A+ from their professor or an *"Atta boy"* from their elite team captain or superior officer.

The reason I make this point is the same reason I make it with the JFK murder. The final shooter, though guilty as sin, is not the point where the conspiracy is conceived, coordinated and covered up... ***that's pure excrement!*** So, by going after the *"lone gunman"* we will always be letting the BIGGEST CRIMINALS OFF THE HOOK! It's long past time to put an end to that or to accept the crooked politician's favorite argument; *"We need to move ahead and NOT look backwards."* **TO HELL WITH**

THAT I SAY! We need to go after every living traitor and give them a FAIR TRIAL and then hang them! *I don't know about you but I've had ENOUGH of their "JUST US" two-tiered legal system and I won't be personally satisfied until these crooks are shitting in their pants* in fear of what true justice looks like and that they are on OUR lists... Okay, please forgive me for this brief rant but my mother was an accounting professional for a major corporation for TWENTY-SIX years. She was a hard working loyal employee who never did anything to harm anyone and I'm sure that most of the 9/11 victims were just as innocent and undeserving of this treachery.

Imagine looking at your own hand writing through a mirror. Is it easier or much harder to read? How come, it's the same handwriting? It's YOUR handwriting! Keep this fact in mind and recognize that as I continuing to work backwards from "Z to A" the defense may try to swing it back in their favor and simply ignore the FACTS. I will still call all the poles by the numbers already assigned but in the final analysis ONLY ONE OF THE FIVE LIGHT POLES MATTER, #5.

Let's explain away a few more anomalies as they relate to these 5 downed light poles:

- First of all let's recall that the government's own falsified black box evidence showed the plane was NORTH of Columbia Turnpike making the approach that would have

48

downed those light poles **impossible** from both an **altitude level** and a **directional approach angle.** Furthermore, all eyewitnesses, whether they were normal citizens like you and I or **expert witnesses** like the Pentagon's own Police Officers **agreed unanimously** that the approach was from the NORTH of Columbia Turnpike... and they did so **twice** in sworn interviews done approximately five years apart.

- Okay, so that begs the question why the poles? How did they get knocked down? This is where we go back to the self-made coffin that our conspirators unwittingly created. Once the explosive charge had been designed and agreed upon they had to do an analysis that included how they were going to cover up THEIR mass murder. Once they came upon the idea of **ONE MORE HIJACKED PLANE** it was simply a matter of coloring in the boxes with the right "evidence" to assure that no one would question it. So some mastermind came up with the lame brain idea to down the 5 light poles to PROVE THE DIRECTION OF THE ATTACK. One big, rather, **gigantic** problem here however; by doing this, by limiting the approach to ONE SPECIFIC height and angle they had just turned their coffin into a shoebox *(a baby's shoebox at that)* and they had inadvertently boxed themselves in to a dead end corner and no one in command saw that coming... or at least no one that wasn't over-ridden by a *superior* traitor.

- No worries, the FBI, the CIA and the rest of our infamous intelligence agencies were standing ready to do their jobs and confiscate all videos, camera or DESTROY any other evidence they could get their filthy paws onto in order to cover this up... just like they did 54 years ago... and just like they do with all of their murders, coup d'états and false flags since the end of World War II.

- Back to the poles. These poles were approximately 40 feet tall and weighed 247 pounds each. **Four** of the poles seemed easy enough. Our theory states that these were torn down and placed by the Pentagon and/or secret service operatives and laid on the ground the night before the 9/11 attack. They were basically out of sight to traffic on the busy streets surrounding the Pentagon. So, of all the tasks *(but one)* were already accomplished and that little charade was among the easiest tasks to accomplish.

- Here's where it gets very interesting... **Enter POLE #5** and cab driver Mr. Lloyde England who deserves a debunking section all to himself and to whom I thank for inspiring this book's title.

The mysterious incidents surrounding Mr. Lloyde England, his taxicab, light pole #5 and the silent stranger:

I must admit that at first I felt contempt for this poor elderly gentleman UNTIL I heard his entire story and took a walk in his shoes. He not only came across as extremely credible but as a wise man, who was simply in the wrong place at the wrong time, whether by pure happenstance or as part of his FBI wife's instruction... Thankfully he was smart enough to stay alive at the time of the 2006 interview conducted in the "**V1**" video. The TN: on his Lincoln was **546-2400**.

NOTE: See the amazing shot of his damaged car *before* the Pentagon roof (was ?) caved in and the same angle afterwards; it looks like another bomb since the damage is so much MORE EXTENSIVE! View: **National Security Alert - 9/11 Pentagon Event** video *(and I suggest using ¼ speed slow motion...)* at: http://www.citizeninvestigationteam. com/videos/national-security-alert Move ahead to 1:00:00 and 1:00:13 in this longer, more complete version of the previously referenced **(V1)** film.

- The government's story is that light pole #5 was hit by the incoming 200,000 pound airliner at over 350 knots and struck the approaching cabs windshield, which approaching from the opposite direction traveling at 40 MPH *(towards the plane)* when the wing struck the light pole and hurled it through the passenger side of Mr. England's windshield and through into the back seat.

- According to Mr. England's testimony (in 2006) *"A quiet man came from a van behind him and helped him pull the* (240 pound) *pole out of the car, whereupon he fell down to the ground, pole on top of him and had to push it off. The driver got back into the van and simply drove away."*

  - OKAY, now that's a lot of BULL-droppings TO CHEW ON at the same time so let's break these down into digestible *bite sized* pieces.

A. I have to add the fact that I don't remember enough of my high school physics to calculate this all out but what I do remember after playing football for many years is what colliding bodies are capable of doing to one another... So I must ask you, does this story make any sense? Let's just do an *Einsteinian thought experiment*... it doesn't have to be exact... just do your best and we'll hire the appropriate expert to see how close we all with our SWAG guesses. Now imagine **YOU ARE THE LIGHT POLE**, firmly planted to the cement base with four steel screws, when a 200,000 pound plane moving at over 350 MPH hits your 247 pound (hollow) body frame that is standing absolutely still. What happens? As the STORY goes that pole (#5) is torn from its base and "allegedly" is thrown into a cab's windshield that is approaching at 40 miles per hour, not that the incoming speed would add that much more force to the already massive amount of energy injected violently into that pole and now heading for the windshield. I don't know what you came up with but I know for a fact that a small man moving very fast can run right over a big man who is standing still. I also KNOW that a good solid hit on a person can send him bouncing for five yards or more. Okay now multiply the mass of a football player by over 1,000 times and increase the max speed by over 20 times and since ENERGY is a function of mass and speed, that is one heck of a hit. So forgetting how many dozens, or even hundreds of yards that pole should have flown, how is it that it is shown lying serenely next to his vehicle?

B. How is it that "IF" THAT POLE had gone through his windshield and was then removed; *(as Lloyde fell backwards with it, whereupon it collapsed upon him)* why wasn't there even a tiny scratch on his

Lincoln cab's shiny hood?   Or any cuts from flying glass?   HECK, why wasn't he beheaded or maimed as his entire vehicle was lifted off the ground and thrown some *(as of yet)* undetermined distance by the MASSIVE FORCES AT PLAY. You see; same old, same old ridiculous TAURUS THE BULL KIND OF GARBAGE.

C. Alright, dissection time.   First of all let's hear what this gentleman had to say when he didn't know the camera was rolling: This isn't exact but it is close and is comprised of both the **V1** short and the extended version referenced above.   It is reconstructed to be as accurate as I can make it with these two reference films: ***"You know what history is?"*** Mr. England says.   ***"You gotta understand what he is saying.   It's not the truth, it's <u>HIS</u> STORY!   It has <u>nothing to do with the truth</u>, it's HIS STORY! This is too big for me man, this is a big thing. Man you know this is a <u>WORLD thing</u> happening. I'm a small man. You know. My lifestyle is completely different from this.   I'm not supposed to be involved in this. This is for other people. People who have money and all this kind of stuff.*** *What do you mean?* (The interviewer asks...) ***I'm not supposed to be involved with this; I don't have nothin".*** So your point is that

54

the people who have all the money... *"This is their thing! This is their event... This is for them."* You mean they're doing it for their own reason? *"That's right. I'm not supposed to be in it."* They used you right? *"I'm in it. We came across the highway together".* You and THEIR event? *"That's right".* They must have planned it. *"It was planned. One thing about it; you gotta understand something. When people do things and get away with it, you, eventually it's going to come to me. And when it comes to me it's going to be so big I can't do nothin' about it. So it has to be stopped in the beginning when it's small you see? To keep it from spreading. This is a rich man's world and these things are done by people with money. I ain't got no money!"* That statement of Mr. England's was one of the most sincere and compelling comments I have ever heard.

D. Let's look at a few things because even in deception there is usually some amount of truth to be distilled. For example; I believe that POLE #5 was in the middle of the road and forced him to stop his cab quickly. What I don't believe is that it had been taken down and laid in the road the night before so I personally conclude that it was detonated to fall just as the plane approached the Pentagon. This just happened to be when Mr. England drove by... or was it? We found out very late in this report that Mr. England's wife worked for the FBI... so that makes me more than a little suspicious.

E. Then a van stops behind him and *"a silent stranger got out of the car and helped him remove the pole, then got back into his van and drove away."* MORE BULLSHICKA mixed with a touch of truth! The airplane hits the Pentagon and they are busy at work removing that pole, then driving away as the building burns?? WHO WAS THE GENIUS THAT THOUGHT UP THAT STORY? Unfortunately, I have to presume for the moment that it was Mr. England's turn to say something stupid. After all, he has probably just had his life threatened by a government agent that immediately appeared from a van behind him and (perhaps) in order to give him something to work with probably took out a blackjack and smashed in the cab's windshield. There is NO WAY ON GOD'S GREEN EARTH that Pole #5 was hyper-driven into any car without massive internal damage to the car seats or frame and thrown with significant force from the point of impact. The agent on the other hand, had finished his job, had time to put the fear of GOD into Lloyde England, smashed in his windshield to give him the start of an excuse in case someone asked him *"who was that man you were talking to?"* Perhaps he was simply told to say a good Samaritan stopped to help, mopping up the only eyewitness that actually saw light pole #5 fall and then simply drove away... a little truth mixed in with a whole lot of silliness. i.e. Would you or I or *any* sane person tamper with the scene ESPECIALLY after just having witnessing a gigantic plane, or at least an explosion at the Pentagon just a short distance away?

Finally: Imagine hitting a baseball solidly with a full swing. Does the ball fall down to the ground in front of the batter? *Of course not!* How is it then that a 200,000 pound plane, travelling over 350 MPH, can hit 247 pound light poles (that stand 40 feet tall) and they are neither sheared off OR thrown a significant distance but merely, according to the government animation, simply *"fall over"*? NONSENSE!

And, why are there NO WITNESSES or photographs showing the pole inside the cab or anyone removing it? (Hint: *There are!*) It seems that this shadow government of ours just loves to muddy up the waters and keep *baffling us with bull droppings!*

NOTE: <u>ALL WINTESSES</u> swore that the plane was NOWHERE NEAR THE LIGHT POLES! Before anyone misjudges Mr. England please listen to his words yourselves since this unfortunate fellow obviously was caught between a rock and a hard place and wanted to live to see another day... I just don't know if his FBI wife got a nice payday out of the scam or if that was JUST ONE MORE COINCIDENCE. See: "**9/11 The Impossible Case of Flight 77** (i.e. "**V1**") at ~34:50 to get the *false view* and the *in between the lines view* from whom I perceive to be an HONEST man who was caught in the middle of a bad murder plot. But then again, I've already said that... but some things are worth repeating. Things like this:

"There is no statute of limitation on murder!"

"There is no statute of limitation on murder!"

<u>"There is NO statute of limitation on murder!"</u> *!!!*

Patience, we're getting down to brass tacks here. So I can hear you thinking: *"Okay smart guy, so what happened to the plane that everybody SAW, even if it was NORTH of Columbia Turnpike.* I'm very glad you asked. Please swear in: **Roosevelt Roberts Jr.** and I will simply tell you what he swore to. But first let me identify Mr. Roberts as *Police Officer Roberts, an expert witness*. When everyone else was either out of view or ducking and running for cover *Officer Roberts SAW THE low flying plane fly away IMMEDIATELY AFTER THE EXPLOSION!*

Let that sink in a moment... Got it? Okay, then let's proceed...

Sound impossible? <u>Hardly</u>! Buzzing buildings is as old as flight itself! Whether or not the aircraft that buzzed the Pentagon was remote controlled or not is yet to be determined but since it didn't have to crash my money places an expert pilot at the controls and not some remotely located stick jockey. It could have been done either way but I sure would love to interrogate that pilot! The aircraft that buzzed the Pentagon DEFINITELY had a course that came from **NORTH** of Columbia, which made the government's approach theory, the one with the fallen light poles IMPOSSIBLE, **just one more proof of THEM lying**. What was it that President Bush tried to say; *"Fool me once..."* (and then he became all confused) Well it continues like this; . . . *shame on you, but fool me TWICE then it's SHAME on me!*

I can envision the government positioning their demolitions person in a manner to determine the proper proximity between the approaching plane and the Pentagon explosion that was to be detonated. It could also have been done by the pilot but I doubt it since that person could have simply changed his mind versus a person with a gun to his head on the ground and backup standing by *"just in case"*. Whoever it was they simply had to press the TRIGGER at the spot that would cause any witnesses to flinch and run for cover so that the plane would have appeared to have crashed and not been seen flying away.

So the prosecution's THEORY is that the explosive charge was **PREPLANTED *and that this was ABSOLUTELY PREMEDITATED MURDER!*** The target was neutralized and all of the evidence from the **2.3 TRILLION DOLLAR THEFT** and the ***ONE HUNDRED and TWENTY FIVE INNOCENT SOULS*** that were callously ***OBLITERATED*** and removed from THEIR equation.

Not a bad deal for the Pentagon, 125 ***CIVILIAN*** lives that they cared nothing about, in exchange for the cover-up of this theft and the probable arrests, trials, convictions, dishonorable discharges, loss of pensions and multitude of sentences ranging from murder and a life in prison, to TREASON and death by FIRING SQUAD! Let's not forget the co-conspirators from the various mop-up teams and all of THEIR SUPERIORS who either were directly involved or turned a blind eye. The photographic evidence disappears into THEIR imaginary black hole, where even light cannot escape, the tapes are all ***"DISAPPEARED"***, with God knows ***WHO*** else and the bought and paid for FAKE TV NEWS and Newspapers, along with all of their complicit owners and PRESTITUTES started wagging their lying multi-million dollar salaried tongues in a ceaseless chorus of deceptive drivel in an all-out attempt to brainwash and befuddle the entire population of the world. ***"You can fool some of the people all of the time, you can even fool all of the*** *people some of the time... but you cannot fool all of the people all of the time!"*

Well guess what ladies and gentlemen of the jury; some of us *were awake*, watching, waiting, listening, communicating and reading declassified documents with open minds. We have been studying each other's research and then doing our own and sharing it with one another over the Internet, which was one thing that the globalists *DIDN'T SEE COMING* nor did they plan for its ramifications! They didn't count on us putting our collective minds together into one super-human-computer that could debunk their endless stream of rubbish in a matter of months, weeks or even days!

Now that we are on to them, THEIR redundant plots and *"INSIDE JOBS"*, now that we have learned to listen to George Santayana's wisdom and *study history* we can recognize the similarities, the recurring rhymes, the REDUNDANCIES *(like THEIR constant destruction of evidence)* so we will NOT have to live through the constant barrage from sociopathic criminals!

"*WE THE PEOPLE*" of the United States *and the rest of the world* have woken up to our Shadow Government's treachery. We have learned that they *are not* the benevolent parents we once thought when we innocently entrusted our children's education, health and future to.

Instead, we have studied the lessons THEY have taught us, albeit the hard way, over these past five and a half decades and we are NOT going to fall for THEIR lies EVER again. When THEIR mouths move we now ASSUME they are lying to us and these criminals will never again regain our trust... ***NOT UNTIL the justice system proves itself to us; NOT UNTIL the rigged election machines are discarded and replaced with verifiable paper trails like so many other <u>civilized</u> nations; NOT UNTIL we see these criminals treated arrested, prosecuted and convicted*** in the same way as the poorest among us with this degree of EVIDENCE! Not until we see the dismantling of the Patriot Acts and the loss of OUR liberties fully restored... ALL OF THEM and if that means turning off the million gallon per day water flow to the NSA's supercomputers in UTAH, then TURN THEM OFF!

We NOW KNOW OF THESE sociopathic lifestyles that have corrupted the very fabric of our Constitutional Republic and it SHALL NOT STAND! No longer will we turn a blind eye to the murderous, drug dealing, war mongering, pedophilia ridden, profiteering FASCIST AGENDA; their "ONE WORLD ORDER" **will fail** because ***WE THE PEOPLE WILL SUCCEED!*** We will determine our children's future and we will determine the future course of our nation without these thugs at the helm... and we will prosper and regain our lost footing as a beacon of light to other nations and not a tyrant with a big stick.

So, as you listen to the choruses of pre-determined and prepared PROPAGANDA on the evening news tonight we must ask ourselves IN ONE VOICE; *what are we going to do about it?* How about enforcing the original anti-monopoly laws and taking back OUR public airwaves!

The criminal enterprise that is OUR government has organized so far beyond our naïve belief systems that even the MAFIA pales by comparison. Don't think THEY wouldn't take you or I or our children and torture us or put them in the ground ALIVE, until you cave in to their demands; because that is EXACTLY what sociopaths and psychopaths do and will continue to do if we don't stop them! THEIR propagandists in Hollywood and TV make up stories about those who torture and try to convince us they are heroes and THEY create false narratives to teach THEIR imaginary history via the silver screen or TV. Remember *"The West Wing"* a great show and IF ONLY our government conducted itself that way... but no, that too was just a pleasant fiction. They try to convince us we're the good guys even as we rape, pillage and are responsible for millions of deaths of innocent men, women AND children! Then we wonder why so many people around the world hate us. Sorry George Jr., it isn't because we are free... it's because we have created these enemies through our own atrocious behavior.

I know there is one more piece of chad on this theory of mine that we have yet to discuss; the misrepresented story of the SECOND AIRCRAFT that was seen at the Pentagon, which was flown by **Lt. Colonel Steve O'Brien**. Colonel O'Brien was indeed in the air at that time over Washington DC. In fact he was the PILOT flying the military C130 aircraft that passed over the Pentagon about three minutes AFTER the explosion and previous fly by. This C130 *was not* the plane identified by the Pentagon Police Officer Roosevelt Roberts, Jr. who swore that *"the fly by occurred immediately after the explosion took place."*

The aircraft that replaced the commercial airliners were military, which explains how they reached such great speeds, maneuvered the way they did and pulled G forces that would have definitely destroyed the civilian aircraft. The military planes did look SIMILAR to the untrained eye to the American Airlines and United Airlines aircraft they replaced. The C130 military cargo plane looks NOTHING like a commercial 757 and the news stories that followed this tragic event were a manipulation by the media to further obfuscate the truth.

What the government has given us is four separate puzzles; WTC towers 1 & 2, the Shanksville crash, the WTC building 7 and the Pentagon attack. In order to maintain their cover stories they have done everything in their power to make our fact finding as difficult as possible. Not only have they given us four difficult puzzles but they have mixed them all into one pile and turned the pieces upside down and then added in a good portion of misinformation, misdirection while trying to conceal or destroy evidence. This has been a sixteen year journey to see this one specific event, the Pentagon MURDERS with what I believe to be *crystal clarity* and it has only been made possible by the thousands of decent men and women who have given tirelessly of themselves to find the truth. Now, standing their shoulders we saw what really happened; that the government's so called exit wound in the "C" ring of the Pentagon was in fact an entrance wound created by a shaped explosive charge. With that one extra dimension added I was able to reverse the chain of events and completely EXPLAIN all of the anomalies that had us stumped... UNTIL NOW! THE PEOPLE'S THEORY is the ONLY explanation that holds true at every juncture and makes sense of what happened at the Pentagon on that fateful day.

As for one important and haunting remaining question that we can now ask without being painted as lunatics: *If the planes didn't crash then where are they?* And *"Where are the passengers?"* We have evidence of two planes doing a *"do-si-do"* and apparently replaced by other aircraft, most likely military aircraft; we have the plane that allegedly crashed into an empty field in Pennsylvania leaving virtually no trace; then we have our Pentagon plane that was substituted somewhere over West Virginia where there was a known radar void. Whether the planes that crashed into the World Trade Centers were drones, as per the Operation Northwood's plan from 1962 recommended, or not, will have to wait for another trial at a near-future date... **"Pilots for 9/11 Truth"** have positively established that the allegedly "hijacked" planes were still in the air long after they supposedly crashed into their targets...

So then where are the passengers and the planes?

That question is one that MUST BE ANSWERED and all I can offer is a hypothesis, another "theory": The planes were landed safely at military bases during all of this confusion and the transponders in each aircraft were turned off, albeit too late since they were followed by radar and outlived the alleged crashes they were involved in.

If I were to take an educated guess as to the whereabouts of the passengers I would say; *"they are doing what they were told they'd be doing and are off living their lives with new identities. Perhaps some are working on top secret projects, perhaps some are spies that needed to be dead to protect their top secret covers, perhaps some were in the witness protection program."* I would lay odds on all of these possibilities BEFORE believing a single word provided by the SHADOW government.

Ladies and gentlemen I wish to thank you for your attention and for reliving this most difficult chapter in OUR history one more time. We look forward to your verdict and trust in your wisdom. God Bless America and God Bless the future we decide to leave to our children.

EPILOGUE:

For those of you who have disowned us, mocked us and made us outsiders among you; *we forgive you.*

We have all grown up under a government that has given itself permission to lie to us, to grant powers to the media that allowed them to consolidate into six companies that together provide over 90% of what we see on TV, read in the newspapers, or hear on the radio. In essence, it is those in power who profit by the false narrative; that my brothers and sisters is a form of government known as FASCISM.

Not only are we taught these lies in "public schools", which more accurately are indoctrination centers designed to breed us into obedient ser-vants *(thanks to corporate entities such as the Carnegie and Rockefeller Foundation)*, who wanted only obedient workers for their factories; but we are also faced with other obstructions, such as our own normalcy biases, natural innocence and desire to believe in a benevolent government.

But *"what if"* the wealthiest families in the world, the 1/10 of 1% used their POWER to infiltrate and corrupt our government, our banks, our corporate institutions and colleges over multiple generations? What if bribes, threats, blackmail and even murder were used in such a sociopathic manner that all but the bravest among our representatives left governing behind and sought out careers that didn't leaving them feeling dirty, complicit or scared out of their wits at the end of the day?

"What if" our "FEDERAL GOVERNMENT" was little more than a huge organized crime family that made the MAFIA seem like a knitting circle? "What if" the war on drugs was nothing more than "*a war on the competitions drugs*" so the C.I.A. could bring in $1 TRILLION dollars a year from the opium fields of Afghanistan to fund their black operations? What if you were a loyal patriot, a soldier, who was ordered to guard those fields and then read about the escalating heroin crisis in the United States? What if you were the parent of one of the 22 soldiers who commit suicide each day? What happens to our precious children who are serving with honor and integrity but WON'T BE bought and sold?

What happens to brave representatives, like Ron Paul or Cynthia McKinney, who gave of themselves tirelessly but were voices in the wind praying for the day when Americans would finally WAKE UP! They become outsiders to the machine and are often destroyed or neutralized by the vast forces stacked against us. Most of them finally give up and leave the government in search of honest employment when they recognize they really couldn't make a difference; or they take the money, shut up and vote along party lines and spend most of their energy trying to feather their own nests or raise money to get re-elected.

Do a quick Internet search and find out how many of OUR politicians hold DUAL-CITIZENSHIP with other countries. Then see which country has more control over us than all of the others COMBINED. This is not the place to go into those details; they will be exposed soon enough as we see WHO set the demolition charges in the three World Trade Center buildings, then cheered for joy when those buildings collapsed and then went home to their country, to their families, loved ones and friends, to speak about their success on public TV and to rejoice publicly in THEIR accomplishment. I'll give you a hint; it wasn't ANY of the countries that we attacked.

But these people were only co-conspirators. They could not act alone nor did they. In this presentation we have only looked at one aspect of the horror that took place on September 11th, 2001; the Pentagon attack. Perhaps now all of the difficult and dangerous work done by a relatively few brave souls has FINALLY culminated into that last straw, the final snowflake that will break the camel's back or bring down the avalanche AND obliterate the ongoing myth of 9/11 and the SHADOW government that conceived, planned, orchestrated and then COVERED UP THEIR ATTROCITIES with the combined power of the military-industrial-intelligence-media complex that was at the very core of this operation.

That is why we must suspend our innocence, our naïveté, our normalcy bias and do what I have done;

and that is to walk in the shoes of the murderers, the sociopaths, war-profiteers, insurance fraudsters and war mongers who all benefited from this singular plan; this *catalyzing event*.

This is a long story and it may take another generation to sort it all out. But today, upon all of those shoulders who have come before, I stand perched and able to see just a little farther. Just far enough to UNDERSTAND that the entrance wound allegedly made by the plane was a fallacy just waiting for one more fact that would allow a concerned citizen to put two and two together and see that wound differently; as a self-inflicted wound using a shaped demolition charge, to murder ONE HUNDRED and TWNETY FIVE innocent civilians in order to cover up the 2.3 TRILLION DOLLARS that was stolen out of the Pentagon budget as announced by Secretary of Defense Donald Rumsfeld on the very day before those innocent lives were taken with premeditation, along with *ALL OF THE EVIDENCE THEY could possibly destroy!*

So what is the purpose of this book? It is to mobilize the citizens of the *United States of America* to stand up and *demand en masse* that the arrests begin, the trials started and then faithfully concluded by Judges and juries that AREN'T bought and paid for by the criminal elite. I intend for this book to be the *FIRST domino that WILL FALL in the 9/11 INSIDE JOB* criminal prosecutions and when felled will bring all of the other aspects of this hideous crime down in procession.

To see truth and justice prevail in the case of September 11th, 2001 will bring closure to those of us who have suffered alongside of the victims over these sorrowful sixteen years. Closure on this ugly chapter in OUR history WILL BE a beautiful thing that will earn us back a modicum of respect that was lost in its entirety from the rest of the world that saw through the lies and suffered from the aftermath of our aggressions. We need to take this first step to change course and travel a different path; one that we will be proud to leave to future generations...

God BLESS America and all

that we should and CAN be!

*"Another world is not only possible, she's on her way.
Maybe many of us won't be here to greet her,
but on a quiet day, if I listen very carefully,
I can hear her breathing..."*

Arundhati Roy

Other works by this author:

"The Judgment"

A Clancy-esque thriller about taking OUR country back.

Written in 2007

"The Children and the Stone"

One poet, one lifetime...

2nd Printing 2013 / 3rd in December 2017

Upcoming:

"One Patriot's Conversation with

America in the 21st Century"

(Available ~ Q4 of 2018)

Visit us at:

"Door to Door"

http://www.palaggio.net

CPSIA information can be obtained
at www.ICGtesting.com
Printed in the USA
FFOW03n0412181217
43992593-43162FF